THE UNSAID PASSING

ESSENTIAL POETS SERIES 131

 Canada Council   Conseil des Arts
for the Arts   du Canada

ONTARIO ARTS COUNCIL
CONSEIL DES ARTS DE L'ONTARIO

Guernica Editions Inc. acknowledges the support of
The Canada Council for the Arts.
Guernica Editions Inc. acknowledges the support of
the Ontario Arts Council.

B.W. POWE

THE UNSAID PASSING

GUERNICA
TORONTO · BUFFALO · CHICAGO · LANCASTER (U.K.)
2005

Antonio D'Alfonso, editor
Guernica Editions Inc.
P.O. Box 117, Station P, Toronto (ON), Canada M5S 2S6
2250 Military Road, Tonawanda, N.Y. 14150-6000 U.S.A.

Distributors:
University of Toronto Press Distribution,
5201 Dufferin Street, Toronto, (ON), Canada M3H 5T8

Gazelle Book Services, White Cross Mills, High Town,
Lancaster LA1 1XS U.K.

Independent Publishers Group,
814 N. Franklin Street, Chicago, Il. 60610 U.S.A.

First edition.
Printed in Canada.

Legal Deposit – Fourth Quarter
National Library of Canada
Library of Congress Catalog Card Number: 2005931744

Library and Archives Canada Cataloguing in Publication
Powe, B. W. (Bruce W.)
The unsaid passing / B.W. Powe. -- 1st ed.
(Essential poets series ; 131)
Poems.
ISBN 1-55071-209-8
I. Title. II. Series.
PS8581.O879U58 2005   C811'.54   C2005-905341-0

CONTENTS

For the lady of the roses

Let Love be the cause
Agrippa

I

A CHILD'S SONG

O the leaves are falling.
The wind breaks the trees down.
O the trees are falling.
The wind is breaking them down.

We will build a home in the trees.
We will climb up with our animals
and build a new home
in the leaves.

We must climb up high
so the trees will be safe
and build our home high up
so the wind will see us.

Then the wind won't break us
but become a friend.
This is what the wind
wants, to be our endless friend.

I

My son and I went crayfish hunting in the creek.
On the other side of town, at the edge of cornfields,
beside the baseball diamond and swimming pool,
we saw women wading in the water, mothers, daughters,
sisters, catching tadpoles and guppies. Beside highgrass
and reeds, the children laughed and shrieked
when crayfish darted away, scrabbling under stones.

Thomas, cranky from the long humid day,
suddenly beamed, as if he'd found inspiration;
he shouted and went to play, his laugh
like some joyful detonation. He joined the girls,
teasing them, made deals for crayfish, following
identical twin sisters from his school under
the footbridge, as if they were his guides.

On the steep bank I sat down and smiled.
The girl's mothers hovered in light filmy dresses
and baggy jeans, in their shorts, t-shirts, some in swimsuits
dripping from the nearby townpool, and we talked
of nothing, really, it was idle evening chat,
though I wished I'd been a cavalier,
offering each of them a rose.

II
Names were offered, girls called Kate and Diana,
the twins Amy and Sue, one named Miranda,
their friends Jen, Jenny, Jennifer and Jean,
mothers, Mary, Teresa, Ruth and Carmen.
Introductions, clarifications, some serious whispering
among themselves, charm and amusement,
as if my son and I had been invited into a garden.

It must have been loneliness, or archaic romanticism,
something, I don't know, that united Thomas and me,
a closure, maybe, deep knowledge of how encased
and confined we can be, silence and separations
haunting us, making us yearn for
some forgiveness, welcome beyond ourselves
into what mystics call the centre of the heart.

III
I saw rainbows
through water mists,
lawns transformed
by arcs of light.

I saw her
in a sunlit dress,
Isis in her eyes,
worlds brimming

in the liquidalive sun –
and I knew
we'd fallen
from gratitude's crown,

yet even here, her, in this town
hieroglyph, herald,
amen, omen,
dreams, secrets,

intimations of the invisible –
the Mystery time
charging us
with waves that are words.

IV
But this is the coldsouls' time
Empire, Imperium –
Rome has won.

Armed ghosts
swarm against
the memory of love.

Lasercool from blacktowers,
power surges
into everyone.

The city appears frozen
by what we gather
in terminals, screenbanks,

like Alexandria with her library burned,
Athens with Socrates silenced,
Jerusalem without David's psalms.

V
I saw her
wearing white
carrying roses

and I thought
she bled
walking along artery ways.

Mourning tears
burned
like illuminated letters

from an ancient
tongue,
premonitions

of grieving
for something, someone –
she, we, had lost.

VI
I shuddered away from provisional streets
to private passions,
and my quicksilver children,

learning, looking
for where hearts
would not stop coming.

And a dream
persisted
like an infiltration

without images
without words
without faces I knew

telling me
people would return
to prophecy's gifts

terrifying holiness
and the sacred
spell

and then who will we serve
and what
will we serve

when Rome has won

VII
A child charged
in a field
revealed light's dance

in his
handling
of the leaf

he pondered
for an hour
and named a flower

VIII
Thoughts of the unborn,
like a whispering
imprinted strangely,

as if they gleamed
like the light seen
before the sun rises,

or like darkness
closing, night
felt around twilight,

We aren't children
in the way
you once knew –

We will blaze
into you
like Damascus heat,

telling all, sleep
with your hearts
wide awake.

IX
Soon the children
will see the wild
and danger
in the garden again.

Soon children
will huddle, preparing
to crusade
beside the towers.

Emanating light
they will see
the global city
burn,

beautiful homes
and churches
in a rain
of sparks.

Soon they will live
through nights
with new songs given
to them.

X
We lingered late by the creek,
my son and I, after the women
had gone, near the baseball diamond,
and the quiet back road.

Thomas gathered up flowers,
midsummer flame and gold,
handfuls then armfuls.
He lay them like offerings

or wreathes beside small whirlpools
swirling up in the cool water,
homages to those who had departed
leaving us alone by green banks,

while I silently watched
the sky and moving stars
throw off the burial of clouds,
and waited for the honey of thunder.

*

I took my restless children to the glittering lake
where so many stars had fallen.
And said, Look at the galaxies,
each star is a soul burning with love,
each star moves and thrives
because of the love that compels them,
each star illuminates the darkness with warmth.
The universe is becoming warmer, not colder,
it's getting bigger, not smaller,
it's becoming more connected, not less,
there's more life to come, more stars, more planets,
more of the grit and desire to live.
Sometimes stars fall into the lake.
They come down to the world, where they roll and unroll
in the rise and fall of the water. Watch the stars
on the crests and surfaces, they've come down
to shine for us –

My daughter whispered, That's a good story.
My son murmured, But what about the moon?

*

The snow fell
like thousands of angels
rushing to a wedding.
The snow surrounded us,
white engulfed us,
while we drove, we three,
down the country road
to the village school,
the old brick home
that enfolds my children,
warmly protecting them.
The snow fell
like legions of ghosts
flying down to rest on the road,
the trees, bushes, farmhouses and cars.
Soon we couldn't see,
we were snowblinded, immersed.
I slowed our car,
and when I did the music soared
on the radio, a slow sorrowful clarinet.
The second movement melody rose,
Mozart's melancholic joy singing,
love travelling across the years.

Katie asked,
Can we stop here and hear this?
I pulled the car over
to a vacant lot, and together
we listened
to that aching soothing clarinet.

My quiet children.
I felt Thomas breathe behind me,
his calm nearwhisper on my neck,
and Katie nestled

watching the white misty veil
of angels and ghosts.

We were lifted, raised by music,
stilled, their reception ardent
beyond their years,
and my love for them
filled the sky
like the snow.

The movement stopped,
inevitably changed,
following the form; miraculously
the snow slowed too.

I asked, Do you want to go now?
I don't want to leave here, he said.
It's all so beautiful, she said. So beautiful.

I lost my children later.
If only for a short time.
My ex came, took them
for a week.
The treaty and truce
of a bloody divorce.
Our children now refugees
of marriage in the millennium,
all of us travellers
on some broken road.

My house never seemed so quiet,
or bare.
The trace of harmony faded,
and I was left,
two parts of me
missing,

asking, if the snow can fall
and music can play,
will our souls ever rise again
to meet them?

*

We walked
in the wet musty garden.
Listen, daddy, my son said.
What is it, Thomas?
I can hear the flowers.
I smiled
then asked,
What do they sound like?
Sshh, hiss, he said.
And what are they saying?
Grow, grow.

I

My daughter lamented, Where's my brother?
Gone for a sleepover at a friend's,
with Katie left to patrol the upstairs hall
like an anxious officer who'd lost her beat.

I forget what he looks like, she said.
I led her by the hand into the bathroom,
and presented her
in the mirror.

Taking a brush, I swept her hair
back, saying, There,
look closely,
you look like your brother.

She laughed, retreated smiling,
only to return
to angrily proclaim,
I don't look like anyone at all.

II

Thomas sat with me at breakfast,
oddly withdrawn,
after his sister had left to spend
a night with their mother.

I tried to get him to speak.
I miss my sister, he confessed at last.
Recognizing an opening,
I asked him why.

Amazement fired his eyes.
Why do you miss her?
Why? He said, shocked.
He thought and thought.

Then preparing to utter
the strictest confidence,
as if he were about to reveal
the Orphic secret,

he leaned forwards,
shook his head
at the importance
of what he was to intimate,

and stared
at me.
Dad, he said,
she's my twin.

*

The stars envied us
while we made love last night.
They streaked through your blinds
like glittering voyeurs
to see us steal their primeval spark –
and make on your sheets a new world
of magnetism and fire.

*

This is how the empire was lost:
all day lolling in scents,
skin luxuriating in skin,
until they became so sore and hungry
they had to rest, nearly blinded by the damp
from their thighs and tongues,

slipping slowly from slippery sheets
into a waiting bath
of milk.

(Look, they said, the eunuchs stare –
they know
of what we're depriving them.)

They seduced one another away
from politics – desert marches, eager legions –
into this sensual reshaping of molecules:
no place now
where one begins
and the other ends.

*

You curled the white sheet around your waist,
pulling it up to your still erect nipples,
and whispered of Adam and Eve
wandering in Eden without names.

Who named them? you said.
Why would names matter in paradise?
They knew the other, and knew God.
What else would they need?

Images from *Last Tango in Paris*
seared into me –
Brando in the bare room's light
declaring, No names here, no names,
to her, as if he needed to fiercely inhabit
the innocent dream again –

You look like the devil, you said,
stirring me from the movie's moment.
The devil? Me?
Your eyes, you said, their eerie green.
You smiled though I was lost
to your brown stare and brown ringleted hair
(I loved her in ways
that astonished me).

I'm no devil, I said.
Then let's pretend, you said,
easing the bedsheet aside
from your nakedness.

*

Put out the light, still the moon,
don't let love pass from this room.

Silence the street, close your eyes,
our room is a sanctuary for sighs.

Don't say I, whisper we,
one soul rises from severed identities.

Come into our bed, eternity's in a kiss,
no worlds are greater than this.

The night must go, the sun return,
here defiant love will burn.

*

I write this with flowers
that don't exist – simulations
of colour and scent,
invisible symbols – of dedication,

hoping you'll take
the bare letters
and transform them
with alchemist's fire

into a burning rose,
every petal a different shade
turned by
your hand.

*

Did you just take me
into the bathroom? I asked
wondering

what was that echo
and stream
over the mobile phone –

Honey, she said,
I take you
everywhere.

*

When you first came
my cat tracked you –
she stared
familiarly,

trailing round rooms
up stairs down
thinking
(no doubt)

*Train me
to claw again,
to lick, hiss
and arch my back.*

*

Radical theology:
I said, I'll do
whatever you want –
Tell me what you want.

Adam, she renamed me,
it's talk
like that
which got us

into trouble
in
the first
place.

*

Someone should kiss you awake in the morning,
stroke your hair while you drift out of sleep.
Someone should worship your dark skin
as if it had the power to order ardor and tongues.

You need a poet because you are the poem
You need a priest because you are the religion
You need a dreamer because you are the dream

Someone should praise you everyday,
blessing sky, earth, fire and water
for making you more exquisite than a tree,
more sensuous than the sea.

Let me be your messenger,
initiate into the Mysterium
of your lips and eyes —

*

In the night she spoke softly,
Open the window,
inhale the earth,

God is roving again
in the world. Breathe
what he's sent,

let the demons go,
let them go back
without our dreams in hand –

She slept later
while I tried to rest,
listening

to her moan and kick
as if to push
something away –

*

Certain dreams mist the eyes

Madame Bovary, c'est moi –
Flaubert's final elliptical remark
on his deathbed – this confession –
the yearning romantic, dissatisfied lover –

He made her more than he could be.
Withdrawn at the end, overthrown
by the solitude he carried inside him,
he saw her beyond the ruthlessness of writing –

but I think his soul had never been anything
other than the restless demanding love
he'd embodied in her – he forlorn,
impractical, caught in thought, dreamy, distracted –

resisting a life without ecstasy to the last.
Other people's being faded, dulled
into vague apparitions,
except for her –

She must have appeared beautiful
in his last dream,
like the hushed sound
of a kiss on closed eyes.

His fiction eludes us more than his memory

*

Katherine, near sleep, said,
I can't wait for the winter
when we can cling
to one another.

I said,
We're clinging
to one another
now.

She said,
I can't wait for long nights,
the dark
and the cold.

It's already
cold,
already dark,
I said.

*

While I slept by your side
my soul did not,
your visionary love
aroused us to our mission,

your breasts wet
with dawn's heat,
our skin still moist
with the night

as if in summer light,
our perpetual season.
I put off the past, present
and future and put on you.

You offered the key
and everything inside me
became wide
and spacious.

But in late morning
my soul in its habit
slept
though I was awake

watching you go,
my fingers and lips
tasting of your perfume.
Your body's

blessing left me,
in darkness, without
your
hallelujah.

*

Was it you
waiting outside my door
about to ring the bell
Was it you
by the front steps
vowing you would return
Was it you
in the shadow
outside my windows
silently hoping
my soul would open
Was it you
calling
when the wind
rustled through the trees
making the branches
tap on my windows
Was it you
saying you would always call
and had always
waited

*

I've driven with you along the familiar night street,
stars passing over the shining hood of my car.
I've talked to you when abruptly you gripped my hand,
reaching across the chasm that divides us.
I've listened for you when I could hardly hear
your voice over the static and chatter.

But once I did hear you say – long ago –
Wake now, human, stir from this street,
stir from your sleep,
wake to the soul, which is love.

You gathered the moon into your eyes
and released it back in a pool of pearls.

Behind this city surely longing still thrives.
We've become travellers, driving up the boulevards,
like bereaved visionaries mourning
the loss of light –

In the slant of the long street that slashes
this city in two, I lost sight of you.
Storefront neon gave no reassuring signature
or symbol, no map or coordinate,

though I thought I saw
love flash
in the distance –

the heart that sends me out again,
searching –

*

Does smoke remember the flame?
Does fire recall the spark?
Does the candle remember the match?
Can two ever be the same in their knowing?

*

And the scent of your skin
your body's imprint in my bed
the strands of your long hair
how you changed mercurial as lighttips on wildtides
your taste your touch your lips your tongue
how you said my name in different tones
how your feet fit into sandals
the trace of perfume in my room
how you smiled at the sun
how you looked when I gave you roses
one yellow one red
the way you swore when you drove your car
your sharp remark when I forgot to call
the way you wept at the door
how you shook your wet hair loose
how your eyes said love
before you kissed me and I surrendered
to this nostalgia
for what almost was
the possibility
of us

*

Then I remembered talking to you,
making love to you,
as if I'd been making love to poetry itself.

You said, But this isn't what I am.
You're inventing me, turning me
into something that isn't
here.

I'd noted in my journal
that if poetry is grace and thrall,
then I have no choice
but to imagine you.

She said, This means
we have to live with your stories
so they become the same
as our time together.

Was she the music
beyond the song,
the story
behind the fiction?

There you go again,
she said,
you can't
stop.

Somewhere between you and my mind's version
of you – a place
where we could meet –

At times I thought I'd been given
images
but not permission
to breakthrough

to the word
which would truly
let me
enter you.

*

I asked Sara to tell me
how she found love
through her hands –

We had a separate world together
for seven years.
He was married, with young children,
and I was married, with young children,
and we loved and never lived together,
and no one knew
but we loved.

How did you know –

He kept staring at my hands
when we met and talked.
He watched my hands
with such a tender eye
I understood that for him
everything I did would always
be right.

*

If I had a rose for you
instead of words,
I'd surely send it,

but pulsing 1s and 0s
electrified
only the sending.

I somehow saw you scan
your screen,
tapping keys

to feel
my words
as if they were breathing.

But no reply came back,
no cybertrace
or hypertrail

though I trolled every file,
clicked find window view
refresh message help.

E-webs
confirm the glow
and link

of abysses,
sites
without end.

Where was the homepage
with her, pixels forming
the program of love?

The soul wired
into datafield
streaks, monitors multiplying

energy's code, like digital DNA –
our minds
in cabled awe – find – run –

I tapped out
to
the screen,

now blank,
and serene,
software hardware quietened,

dreaming
of other
leads –

*

Night: cold air
of a faroff room,
another city archipelego
run by the strangeness
of anonymous owners –
neon acronyms, satellite dishes,
the screen leaks sensations –
the promise of infinite access –
phonelights flash
questions about my stay,
and I miss
the prayer
and ache
of her sleep.

*

Eyes so bright
in spite
of the wounds
in her body –

She cried out for haloes,
light from the other side,
when she curled up
beside me.

I
After a long day I went outside
to pray, but my back yard
seemed like a desert.
The sun beat down.
I looked, and couldn't find
what love had once done.

The wind rose, scented by mown grass
and apples.
Then the trees began to bend
as if seeking to kneel.

Maples and poplars leaned,
allowing light to reach the flowers,
soil, bushes and grass
beneath them.

Cedars and birches stood upright
and strained
down again
as if to hear
words buried
in the earth.

Branches crackled, heaved slightly,
leaves hissed
like a rush of rain
on a tin roof.

Trees in holy offering,
leaves a whispered sacrifice,
the ground an altar of roots –

II
Once wild sleet pelted this town,
and it was like a supernatural war:
hail smashed branches
on the roof of my car
cracking the windshield
into a crystalline fracture –
splinters like a glasswork's web –
O the cost,
I was furious at the cloudburst,
the old tree
and my stupidity
for leaving my car
in a space
so vulnerable.

III
All around me leaves are falling,
stripped by the wind,
though it isn't autumn in the country –

Willows sway,
though no storm looms today –

And I'm beginning to believe
I may translate the hush
in rain
and leaves,
in supplicant trees:

fall to the wind,

and, if you can,

crack.

*

I dreamed about Thomas Merton,
last Sunday, after church –
strange, even troubling,
I'm still sorting it out.

Friends were there, all of them kind,
and you among them, but I was trying
to speak, and I struggled
with the old words and new words.

Somehow the new wouldn't come.
Something in me kept rushing forward,
even though no one wanted
to hear it.

Like Benjy Compson
trying to say
trying
to say

You vanished –
I found myself alone in a factory.
The colours were autumn rust.
There was a great silence.

With
words
that would not
be said yet.

*

Shatter me – place your hand
on my heart, angel,
don't leave without the sound
of beating wings,
let your bleak tear fall
and raw breath tear
through my house
where I've been asleep
for years –
hurl this soul into fire,
song, praise, ecstasy, sacred air –
dangerous angel,
rain down your command

*
you
you
you

make me

bleed

*

The Master looked from east to west,
then held his forefinger and thumb
to the sky.
He made an inchwide interval
between them, and said,
We are this far from paradise,
only this far.

One inch keeps us
from what you would name
the cherubim,
the flaming sword,
the tree,
the golden rivers,
Eden.

A mere inch,
he said.
But that interval
appears
unbridgeable,
impossible
to cross.

*

Bless stillness
quiet finer and larger
than my self
Bless the quiet
stilling distraction
mind emptying
turning to sky
Bless darkness
stealing in slowly
embracing me
Bless the gift
of speaking silence
Bless the moment
stillness steadies
like the guiding palm
my naked yearning
Bless sleep
awakening
into the calling
of night

*

In the afternoon I finished writing.
I'd had a good day, getting it right on the page
once (at last),
and I headed upstairs,
true to my old habits.
I looked for signs of life,
children, home from school,
whamming cupboards, their laughter,
running, arguments,
all the keen hungry questions,
and found no one there.

O my daughter, my son

Where are you now

O my son, my daughter

When the wind began to build
our names were lost

*

I need a prayer
for what could be there –
to speak one kind of penance
for being
too transparent or hollow,
letting everything through –
blank impressive air

Only yesterday
I was overwhelmed
by infinity –
immensity overcame
facts, fear –

Coming to prayer
I couldn't remember
where I'd begun –

my soul stammers
for darkness – some part –
of eternity

*

The Canada geese this morning –
their V a darting arrow
like an eye opening
to catch the light.

Did you hear them pass
over your house,
the calls like a celebration?

Where do they go when they fly
beyond our sight?
Where do they go,
their cries like fading laughter?

If I had eyes to see
beyond morning,
my horizon like a net,

maybe I could follow them.
They pass
like the people I love
better than myself,

and I can't see
to what skies
they've flown.

*

If trees, clouds, rain and sky
spoke
would their stories be ours or theirs?

Would they talk about
children and love,
ecstasy, tragedy,
disappointment, loneliness –

or would they talk only
of themselves,
our errant concerns
mere background noise?

Stars, planets, comets, dust,
electrons, particles,
fields, waves,
unbroken energies

making remaking
seas, forests, grass, sand,
animals and insects,
speaking to one another,

cosmos of luminous communication
saying nothing
of the human.

*

Could I pray to you,
pearl incarnation –
confess to you,
silversphere in horizon's depth.

If I could, I wouldn't feel
lost, I'd think of you
as if you were the goddess,
lady of the lamp,

my ivory cloister,
nightflower glow,
white secret who inspires
those on the cusp

of holy language –
I'd implore you
because I need to awaken
something –

lunar sheen
like the lighting
of the way –

*

Genesis says God moved upon the face of the waters.
What if that reflection is embedded there,
what we see each time we gaze down into seas,
lakes, rivers, creeks, ponds, pools, falls,
the everlasting imprint in waves –
undulations, transformations,
gray, blue, green, diamond, glitterings
on the horizons, silverblue, whiteblue,
foam, tides, caps and currents.
Stillshape of one always altering,
when we look, withholding our terror,
the thing which most resembles
our moving
selves.

*

In the end
Pascal wrote of the wager
of faith
in immortality.

But of what God's bet
on our striving
mortality?
In the beginning

did you know
the cost of loving
what you started,
that when you rolled the dice,
the supreme gamble
might be lost –

that loving
might never be
enough?

Hours I wonder
if God prays –
nearer
than we know –

hoping we will hear
and accept
petitions
for our forgiveness –

*

My daughter drifting around midnight
as if in some tiny disturbed haunting,
shook me from my light sleep.
Talk to me, I want to talk, she said.

Startled, I felt something
sourceless, engulfing,
and I lunged up
from the dark, shivering.

What Katie, I whispered, what's wrong?
She shuffled close, and replied
Do you worry
when you miss us?

A strange thought to send her out
wandering our house
so late. Yet I heard the urgent
question.

I couldn't stop my thoughts –
these nights were too long
and sometimes the dark
didn't end.

I wanted to say –
though not really to her –
the morning
doesn't know how to come back.

She whispered,
Know what? Thomas is your son
but I'm your sunshine.
A gentle non-sequitur.

I smiled at her precocious wordplay –
though I noted the slightly jealous edge
in the line – and saw her
smile back.

I walked her to her room,
passing by her brother's bed
where he slept, cradled
among toys and books.

Katie fell asleep immediately,
and I shut out her light,
and went back down the hall
to my room

returning to my bed
and the waiting dark,
wishing
I believed in sleep –

*

I pray for no reason
other than to pray
and make the darkness
warm

I pray each night
for the reason
there may be
no reason

*

My son woke up yelling in the night.
When I got to his bedroom,
he was sitting up in his bed, terrified,
speaking as if he were chanting –

I see monsters coming out of the fire,
ghosts staring from the moon,
the tiger leaping for my sister and me.

I tried to reassure him,
There are no monsters
and the fire won't burn you.

But he shook his head and insisted –
The tiger is dreaming me.
My mouth is full of fire.
I don't want to sleep, I can't.

I wanted to offer comfort,
tell him I know about the tiger,
the moonlight like ghosts.

Instead I lay down
on his still small bed,
and we gradually fell toward sleep,

while I hoped the dreams
that possessed him
would pass.

*

Teach me
not to want anything
not to need or be
anything
to be still
not to cry out for more
when there is
no more

Give me a lesson
in light
how to grow
into light

Teach me
to see nothing
so the longing
stops
and I'm still
waiting

Teach me how heaven
could be here
about the other
who follows
that silence
that trace

Teach me love
how to keep
every night
before me
how you sounded
when you stepped
into the garden

Teach me the shadow
and seal
of your solitude

*

What gives you peace?

the promise like a prayer
stillness will rise in the moment
I shut off the ignition of my car
and step out the door

What was it you heard?

the wind at the windows,
shifting ground under the floor,
this unsettled house trying to settle,
the sudden storm over the roof,
a crackling in the air
that may have been the sun
sliding out from behind gray clouds
in its longing for blue sky

What was it you once heard?

a note struck distantly,
the beginning of Eden's melody,
a song heard between the notes
of other music,
a somehow familiar harmony and beat
that made me pause
when I tried to recall their origin

Tell me what moves you?

something that no longer needs
words or images
like the wind roaring
as if it carried a soul or spirit
toward my home and this town,
to our frustrated preparations,
endless and minute,
for tenderness

*

in a dark time
I looked
for an answer –

one note
came – sound
almost unheard

then silence
nearly comforting –
stark sound again

and silence
the rest
within

II

BEATRICE, DANTE

I
She saw him
possess her
with
a stare,

and dreamed
of being followed
by him beside
church walls.

When she clutched
her nightsheets,
her body
damp,

did she pray
this stranger
would free her
from her youth?

II

He prowled Florentine back alleys,
hunting for her, aching for one more glimpse
(as I have, in the town near my house,
when I lost sight of you).

He must have planned the poem
to rival the cathedral he passed every day
after he saw the outline of her form
under her flowing dress.

He stalked her to serve her –
seize the image, paradise
his compulsion –
shuddering mind

engendered by lush hair,
her lips
his confessional –
vision the only way out.

SONG FROM EMILY DICKINSON

I
In my heart – I keep turning
In my heart – I keep
In my heart – I keep turning
and turning away
In my heart –

II
No one appears at my door
though sometimes I hear
the rap –
the whispered name –

but no one lives here,
there's just a house and its fame
for the soul who walks.

III
Who could be that ghost
which haunts the winding staircase
and every room?
What spectre will you meet –
hovering between worlds?
In one life the loving host
with a heart full of children,
another lived in secluded rooms
where you barely see
the elusive shadow
in the window –
slipping between the panes

and the crack
in the nearly closed curtains.
I'm that apparition,
fading at morning –
at flesh's first touch –
fleeing the knock at the door,
craving invisibility,
unredeemed, unredeemable,
anonymous, absurd.

IV
Yesterday, long ago,
you called me romantic,
a lover – and made an end
that was also the start –

Music played,
bells from somewhere,
heaven, hell
sang together.

I'd become reception at last –
an ear –
I had all but disappeared
solaced by solitude,

transmissions – mystery,
intimations
and ruin.

Here, I'll prefer
the transgression of sound
(though ghosts don't speak –
they watch
from a balcony –

listen near
the slightly ajar door –
they leave traces
of their steps
in the dust)

always – and only –
the soul's roar

V
I will leave you knocking at the gate
like a curious wind
baffled at its inability to break in,
and I will climb my staircase
rising alone,
steady and sure the sight
of the lamp I hold
guiding me back
through the darkness,
my home.

VI
Still you once said
when we fled
from the rain
we could be
brave, true –
I haven't forgotten
and can't forget
you still
the one who almost
got through.

VII
in my heart
in my heart – I keep turning
and turning away –
in my heart – I keep
in my heart – I keep turning

*

Seize
desolation,
dust –

welcome
wind,
inhuman hum –

clasp
emptiness
where

the only rain
will be
tears –

in
loneliness
wilderness –

bind, appall yourself,
like the iron gate
locked shut

ISABELLE RIMBAUD

Marseilles,
November 10 1891

You arrived demanding a home,
no one to welcome you,
stranger than the sun,
more a fable than real.

You wrote for demons,
claiming magic and music,
an eye in the dark,
now wanting a hand to hold.

You squall from your bed,
the amputation more to your soul
than your skin,
saying you want to return to song.

Why would I want it?
You have harmed me
with your guns and slaves,
raving and blasphemy.

I hear the unholy in you,
Satan and God mixed up,
white lips murmur
a legacy of secrets.

And I would trade mystery
for food, exchange rants
for rent. We need something
other than words.

Isabelle,
you utter my name,
and I reply take the cup
and cross, redeem yourself

over these sick sheets
and your urine stains,
be loved rather than legendary,
furious, broken and feared.

Never will I listen,
though I will sleep beside you,
comfort your brow, offer my hand,
and whisper in your ear goodbye.

SONG FOR THE SUPERMAN

The Via Po, Turin,
January 3 1889

I wasn't given tears, only toil.
The lash and harness my life.

No stall for a home, streets are my grass and path.
Each day I feel myself becoming slower,

the stones coming closer, the voices more hectoring,
the cold words sting my back.

My muscles are strapped,
though I remember a quick morning

when mere sight of the sun
was an invitation to race.

Now the coachman beats me,
claiming his god's anger,

demanding more work from me,
more effort, pull, obedience and strength,

with no rest,
each day an ending without reward.

Suddenly he was there, dishevelled, shivering,
clothes so ragged he could have been naked.

Not like the others, he wept,
shouting to the whip I barely felt.

His face close, that warm fleshsmell,
his arms around my neck.

Startled, I stamped and reared,
raising my head, almost noble again.

He embraced me,
his voice pitying.

O my brother.
He. Human.

I wasn't given tears, but behold
the man crying out for me,

though he appeared too late,
his weeping too late.

*

White sheets covered her neck
like a blanket of white roses.
He watched her breathe slowly,
and he was sad
beyond words.

When she stirred, slow and still halfasleep,
in subdued voices
they spoke in the hospital quiet.

I'm tired, she said.
What will I do, he said,
when you're gone.
You'll go, and go, she said,
and make what you do,
and have always done,
when you worked, without me.

He watched her, looking for words again.
When you pass on
to the other side, he said,
will you send me
a sign to let me know
that you are safe?
Will you let me know
you've found your way
to the other side?

Her smile was weak, and she only nodded,
almost imperceptibly.
When I'm gone, she said,
I'll send you a single leaf.

Look for me
in a leaf,
and you'll know I'm alright.

Then she said she had to sleep.
And he sat by her bed
for a long time.

When his wife died
it was November,
and there were no leaves
in the countryside
where he lived.
Winter came, and went.
And he went on,
in his empty house,
making things
in the way she said
he would.
He didn't look for signs,
and there were no leaves.

When he finished his work,
he walked around the town
where everyone was left alone
if they so wished.

Spring came early.
The smell of the earth was rich.
After his work one day
he walked and came
to the cluster of flowering trees
where he liked to pause
and contemplate things
on a bench

someone had bought
and placed there
for all.

The wind came up,
and his thoughts strayed.
The magnolias rustled.
Suddenly he was showered
by petals.

He looked up
into the fine rain
of flowers,
and he thought,
they could be leaves.

They fell and fell
on him, and over the fields.
There were so many,
falling like a covering
that obscured
the earth,
a white blanket
on his upturned face
and wet eyes.

THE WOUNDED HANDS

Yo no quiero más que una mano,
una mano herida, si es posible.

...a Spanish princess, who, when she grew old and wizened,
    allowed the court painter,
the official artist of the realm, to capture on canvas
only her hands, which had remained tender, unblistered,
unblemished – the reminder and sign of her
original personality...

I
When will I see your hands? she asked her mother.
Not now, not yet.
I've worn these gloves
since the fire that widowed me

singed them, almost consumed them.
I don't know if you could stand
the sight,
the terrible scarring from the flames.

Her daughter still entreated her,
Let me see your secret hands.
No one she knew
had ever seen them.

Always her mother replied,
Not now, not yet.
But when, her daughter asked,
when will I be ready?

When you are inflamed by love,
someday,
then I'll show you,
but not until you love truly.

II
The girl grew, until
she met a man,
after many boys,
who sparked wonders in her.

They made each other new
every day, discovering
the taste and touch
beyond society.

I'm ready to see
your hands.
I'm ready
because of love.

Her mother, pale, wrinkled,
tired, thin,
sighed to see the ache
in her daughter's face.

Prepare yourself,
she said.
Sit
near me.

Slowly her mother removed
one glove, then
the other, and revealed
white immaculate hands.

The two shuddered
at their otherworldly beauty,
the still youthful hands
that could mold generations.

So you see,
she said, turning them
as if they were a fugitive
mirage,

why I can never,
and must never,
show them
to anyone else.

Few could bear
such grace.
Few could bear the tragedy
of such a vision.

SONG FOR CLARA SCHUMANN

Every note I played, every beat followed,
every chord where I lingered, every overture started,
every ballade I shaped, every phrase traced,
every downbeat set to ignite the whole,
every conversation between cello and piano,
every call and response between oboe and viola,
every symphony a whisper across sheets,
every concerto a walk down a forest path,
every fortissimo leap recalling our dance,
every crescendo grasping for hours and sky,
every coda meant to draw harmony to a close,
every diminuendo and pianissimo a fading goodbye,
every silence a gesture toward the unknown and new,
every sound a passage to love, to you.

SONGS OF CATHERINE BLAKE

London, near the Surrey Shore,
April 1828

I
You saw archangels sing
in a tree,
armies of seraphim
on a Soho street.

I didn't see the spirit,
only trusted your eye.

What is real, you sang,
are cherubim and angels,
what we descend
to after is the dream.

Mr. Blake needed to spend more time on earth,
our patron said.
He should have thought more about being realistic.
Mr. Linnell, Mr. Palmer, were said to be painters too.

But William, you saw light around faces,
and heard your dead brother speak,
because you said the real is the snare
for the soul.

I didn't understand, faltering,
but believed you,
though your words
fell away from me.

If I had the gift
If I could have written or painted
If I could have seen

II
Weigh my heart
with love

Summon me
by night

O melt
the dawn

All should heed
the sweep

of song
through you

William, you called me Albina,
Aubade, then England,
not Cate, nor Catherine,
though I asked
you to say
my name
just once,

which you did, afterward smiling,
and calling me
river river.

Now you sing
the stars,
the eternal gleam
in your dissent reveals
the soul's line
in light.

And I remember how I didn't speak at first,
when you began your song,
I couldn't answer
but I cherished
the vision,

loving your eyes
that didn't get their glow
from me.

III
Years back when the wind
bent the top of the trees
by the cottage we had,
you called to the rain

as if the heavenly host
had come.
For whom do you weep?
you hurled at the storm.

You turned and saw me
cry, frightened.
You wiped the tears
from my cheek

and called them our dew.

And when you returned
I thought to comfort me
and remember our love,
you gave me riddles,

or were they prophecies
of some infinite dare?

You said,
We will become who we are,
history has gone on behind our backs,

Joshua Jesus in you in me
all the cosmos struggles
to allow our selves to be.

Listen,
here's the news:

The tomb is empty,
the heart is full,
go free,

in patience, peace,
fearlessness and ferocity,
go free.

William, I didn't understand you.
Here was a voice

I'd never heard before,
much like yours, surely reminiscent.

You said, I will speak
over the stones
of death.

IV
They come to hear about how you
talk through me.
How can I explain that you say
my golden river, Cate, flow on.

If I could I would
but my sight and voice fade,
and there is only this bed
where your heart once passed over mine.

You brought myths they tell me,
but it was the certainty
in your blessing
touch

that made me want to stay
in our two close rooms.

Now I dream
of an entrance to heaven,
and you open the gate
no one sees

and you step
away from the hearth
no one else knew,
and tell me

Exult, you are
in yourself
Jerusalem,

Though I'm left to tell our patron,
Mr. Blake's gone again to Paradise.
He will be back shortly.

ARK

Cling
to my wreck
gasp in waves, rain –
bewildered
(what had I done?) –
you pass,
torchlights glitter,
voices raised in praise –
the saved
accompany me –
while I sink down
in
their wake

TABOR

Why a glow on that mountain,
a fire without tinderbox trees
or straw?
Why this light just before night?

Perhaps angels, snared sparks,
perhaps the phoenix, something
that wants us, needs us.

Why did wild birds whirl
like a crown of wings
over each being
curled like a shocked fetus –

Strange: eternity's monument,
or just momentary light,
air radiant
like a lightning rift,

perhaps the gift
in seeing, not possessing –
if this could be
our present –

Why did the wind carry
the tongues
of the sun?

GETHSEMANE

Grass, stunted trees,
ancient shrubs, roots
wonder
at the desperate word –

His plea
washes ground

Leaves stitched
to branches –
without doubt's
needle –

SONG OF SAINT FRANCIS

In the morning, sudden to this sleeper, I woke to revelation.
Apocalypse came to me, I was singled out, singed,
lightshafts cracked this unshaped stone, my bounded soul,
and I couldn't grasp it, I didn't know how to speak at first
but I saw a cross.

In the sky it stood against bloodred clouds
mobilizing to obscure it, blot it out.
I saw a cross but it wasn't a key,
or the shepherd's embrace,
or an initiate symbol of suffering,
an ancient cipher somehow reborn.

It was a handpressed against time itself,
against cloud and sky, their furious resistance,
a hand outstretched, and in its nakedness
I saw the word
Mercy

Mercy – to stop cruelty
Mercy – to prepare our hearts
Mercy – to grieve us into gentleness
Mercy – to those whose minds are mean and clouded

And I knelt under the arrival.
Burning above me, set high, the lighthouse hand
showed a celestial scroll

Keep sweet rage and boldness
to oppose murderous oaths and the awful numbness
of brute machinations.
The open hand somehow said,

Stop death,
be ready instead
to hold, caress.

Then I was released from history,
the prison of today, all nature loosened,
light poured, and I was drunk with mystery,
became listening part of the cosmos,
my heart charged, living with the unity
of a newborn mind.

Roses erupted in prayer, beseeching the air.
An infinity of blue sky, abruptly cloudless.
Ageless children darted and laughed
from behind bushes and shrubs.
Trees, furrowed like old faces, looked
to the stars made visible in morning light.
Deep in the forest wolves howled for the lost,
who began to track back, scenting home.
Birds leapt from branches like slaves
unexpectedly freed, disclosing
their songs' secrets
in a new reign of gifts.
All melody and harmony clear to me.

Because the open hand means eternal exposure

Because the self's joy means loss of the self

Because the light and the dark have joined

Because the passwords of the cosmos are sympathy
and justice

I want to live
skinned on the path that keeps radiating
so I may keep falling,

I want to live so nothing hides
and I'll see the soullight always glimmer
near the surface of all flesh,

I want to stay raw
in the mad alleys
of the new Rome.

*

Once I slept under the liberty tree,
and woke – to think I could be free.

So enslaved, as if we cower in Egypt again
though its miracles ask us to snap our chain –

III

*

I'm lucky if the twins sleep in past seven.
Suddenly they're singing, muttering, quarreling, yakking
at toys, out windows (if it's warm), at Chili, our cat.
They romp up and down the secondfloor hall –
Katie's firm tread pounding the ground –
Thomas, a big boy now, yet gentler,
almost silent in his pace.
Everything is a shout.
Let's play, he clamours,
while Katie cries
I'm hungry, like a halfstarved waif.
Excited, they make
the morning
teem.

I wake to this new day chaos,
delightful drift of seeing
what we may discover

in pancakes I'll pack
with blueberries and peaches,
in orange juice slurped up
in circuscoloured straws,
in the bluewhite light
of rural sky,
in the world coming
to our call.

*

Katherine, there was a scent of you
in the fall breeze –
impossible – your perfume –
mingled with pine and willow leaves,
as if you'd walked
along this passageway before me.
I breathed deeply – deeper –
lingering, hoping
I could conjure you
back
in that air.

*

A place he goes to in his mind
belonging only to her,
consecrated ground
for his seared scared heart.

He would tell you
it's a loving refuge
where they arrange the roses,
clean up the dinner table,
blow out the candle –
with cries from their bed
and moist spots
each want to lick up
on the sheets –
where the darkening day ends,
and her radiance begins.

It's only a promise,
this trace
of her touch
and beauty

in the site
he searches for
when things go bad:
there

she shakes her hair
full of curls,
and pads barefoot
across the exposed floor.

*

Love is invisible
yet I feel it in words
as if the pulse were braille

offering a path
to where the heart's
wounds may be staunched

I
She said, You were the soul in the willows
watching over my passion.

You stood by the vine swing
nudging me toward earth.

You were the soul by the river
warning me of hidden undertows and tides.

You stood by the ruined tower
whispering of another route.

You were the soul at my bed's foot
urging me toward peace.

II
She said, Since I was a child
you've murmured
close to my ear.

Since I was young you've placed
yourself between me
and the ravening storms.

You were what I searched for
in the squall.

You were the one I followed
into the tangled pathless garden.

You were the dreamshape
sleek with silver rain.

III
The myth said,
when God walked
through their garden
they cowered

terrified –
by the thunder
in his step –

But what if that God
walked spellbound
at the love
he found –

made the comfort
of seeds and suns,
dreaming of the two
entwined without him.

IV
Under the sun's
fresh alarmed glare,
after the pardon,
in free air —

God watched
over Adam's
dreamless sleep —
no past to draw on —

in Eve's bare arms,
longing to enter
that nakedness
with them.

I
I write in the dark –
a lazy refusal
to turn on the light
turned into a code –

When I can't see the words,
their pull is strong, strange,
beyond my eye,
at the pen's edge.

II
Masses of
satellite bowls

like postulants' hands
cupped to beseech

and receive
waves and light:

new sacred instruments
enfold us.

III
In memoriam: Joseph Amar, 1954-2001.
Images looked for him.
They surged quickly,
flowing up from the canvas
off the floor into his brush
as if he had roused the elements,
while he circled
in an eerie ritual mime

of Jackson Pollock's
balletic twostep.

Forces and presences, he said,
over things.
He provoked energy,
more energy,
drawing his sources
from the ground –
as if his canvas was a screen
for whatever rose and riled the air.

Premonitions of the invisible –
his paintings surprised
the sun.

IV
Amar once asked,
What makes you think God is a person?
Why not a colour? pure red, or blue?
a streak like a comet's tail on the nightsky?

The cross at the centre of a canvas –
the bridge across forms.
Light in background –
a ray like a thoughtcluster.

V
My visionary teacher long ago probed,
Was I from the third world
or from the fourth?

I was from Canada,
I said solemnly.
No, he spoke vehemently.

That isn't what I mean.
From where do you see and hear?
From what point do you begin?

I think now he meant
three dimensions are
not enough.

VI
They hinted at illumination,
(the cities have no darkness)
spiralling knowledge –

Everything must break to open

New worlds burst
at night
after meditation
and experiments

Acquire the habit of resurrection
every day

Sail on
craving keys to secrets –

Invitations to sacraments
glimmer around you –

VII
The winter wind
slams my house,

unlike any wind
I've heard before –

It smashes against
my kitchen's glass door

with a howl
to make you forget

the June
breeze.

The wind
belittles my home,

as if it's warning me
you are

more on your own
than you know.

I think: the wind
needs people

to batter,
forcing us

to build houses
and stand

against
it.

VIII
Sometimes I'm afraid
of the wind, she said,
when a gale crashed
from the west.

My house moaned
like an explorer's ship
tossed at sea.

The elements must be free –
lightningrainwind
thunderhail –
all free

beyond human origin
and hungry
angels –

IX
You said, In Eden
what did the wind
feel like?

What was the taste
of
an apple?

Did we see
what the moon
sees?

Did we understand
what a cloud feels
when it moves?

Did we dream
what animals dreamed
when they twitched in their sleep?

Did we live with the beauty
of various realms
awake in our eyes?

X
Every home has a spirit.
My old house in Ashburn was forlorn.
It gave a sense of being somehow bruised,
standing apart among bright new century homes,
their facades glowing like newly-minted money.
That house obscured by willows, shrouded among maples,
its roof looking leaky, its surfaces cracked,
in need of the loving
it never received.
The house seemed hurt, its pride damaged,
by what – I have no idea –
its history lost to me.
I hated it in rural suburbia at first.
Away from Toronto, the shouts I'd heard,
the shift I'd invited into myself,
that house didn't feel like a home.
My marriage staggered, then finished,
and our twins were dislocated,
worried about where they were to live.
The walls almost sagged to see us.

But when the house became temporarily mine,
until we sold it (at a loss),
I sensed a change in the place.

Kabbalists call
the wind
ethereal waters.

At night when Katie and Thomas slept,
or had been whisked to their mother's,
when the wind converted the leaves
on the trees
into waves, my home
started to find
its sway
of speech.

After I moved down the road
to Stouffville, another young family
(presumably resolved
to stay intact)
bought the old house,
and I hoped it would slowly
let them know –

walls are porous,
the true shield is light,
a house only becomes home
when you've heard its cry –

XI
Here the wind shows off
its riddling spree –
sweeping up dust, twigs,
in small tornadoes –

The wind can be a breath held
in suspension –
you sense the hush
in the landscape –

as if it has retreated
to reclaim
the momentum
behind this world.

XII
Radio waves load the air

Come out
of yourself
and burn

Come out of yourself
and taste the singe
on your tongue

Come out of yourself
your flesh will ravish
the dark

New faiths engulf us –

our answers
like the tapping of prisoners
in silenced cellblocks
morsecoding back
their needy
raps on walls –

XIII
Switch on your mantic screen,
radiance like a waving
day or night.

Catch
the elemental pulse,

the cosmos
seeking portals
of entry into eyes, mind.

No need for SETI –
already apocalypse
strobes –

In the gleam and keystroke
universes
commune.

XIV
Before we came to these worlds,
we had to finish with the other

Before we came to this passion,
we searched for omens and signs

Before we came to ecstasy,
preparations had been long underway

XV
Admit: I can't get over the idea
that when I write
I'm at war with what we call
reality's will.
My children brought
loving back,
and so did
you —

Yet sometimes
I step into night
and ask
for shadows,

closing
my eyes
to feel ground
beneath me,

and sense in the stars
their simulacrum
spin.

XVI
The storm thundered by
and I unlocked the glassdoor
in my kitchen, and walked
into the snow,
the sky suddenly streaked
with rainbows.

My neighbours came out, staring,
shaking their heads, smiling
at one another across fences and bushes.
Imagine that, one said, all those rainbows.

It was as if the sky had ignited
in prisms,
the cold had been infiltrated
by spring.

XVII
I turned on the radio –
Mahler's Rückert lieder played,
every note pitched
to the heart –

God don't flood me with more –

The door
slammed wide,
lightness edged morning

with a beauty
clearer, truer,
than I could
hold –

XVIII
After the door swung in the wind,
after the thaw,
and the eaves spouted and leaked
like ruined fountains –
After the sites and datascreen
went dim –

After memories and mantra air –

Tea steeped in my white mug.

Time spent cooking supper
for myself.

Empty the washing machine,
smooth and fold clothes.

The noisy grit of my old vacuum cleaner.

Time spent alone.

All that stables me.

No one withstands
the ecstatic
for long.

*

Today I write
between stops,
children, teaching,
driving, shopping
(the domestic dad,
not much the stuff
of romantic dreams),
a moment caught,
relief coming
from letting words fall
where they will
on the page
I've torn haphazardly,
groping my way
toward a new
communion.

Tired but amazed,
needing this time,
I want to see
what word comes next,
living as if I'm free
to go along
with morning,
noon and night,

recognizing
how much I love
the mayhem
of my pen.

*

Upstairs Friday morning
I was dressing
and I heard my son
hollering –
not just bawling
but hooting
and whooping –
his voice climbed
up and down the scale,
a wordless howl
like a broadcast
or hawking
between silent homes.

I ran downstairs,
thinking he was in trouble,
swung out the door
and breathlessly shouted,

What's wrong?
Noting the gulls,
robins, blackbirds
and bluejays
assembled around him.

Thomas peered back at me,
nodding his head
as if to say
the problem
is your perception.

Nothing's wrong,
he replied,
I was just talking
to the birds.

*

This Jane Austen revival in the movies may not be a good sign:
all that false politeness, imposed civility and deference,
the cultivated social distance, dependence on inheritance,
tact masking sensitivity, decorous acceptance
of limits, rage jailed in cool humour;
love at best cordial respect, at worst convention, or convenience;
all that fear hence worship of money –

what will future lovers say?

If Emily Brontë were back, Cathy and Heathcliff roaring rebellion,
lust and vision disturbing the rites of great houses –
lightning love welding immortal union –
I'd find things a little more promising.

*

Startled, Diane said, after we nearly collided
on a street downtown,
friends absent from one another for more
than a year –
You look alive,
refreshed,
you must be
in love.

Happy to see her,
my friend impelled
by witchcraft and demons
– she had disappeared into a book,
writing it for a decade
to make one visionary burst –
I said,
In love?
Yes, with life –

I cringed, embarrassed at sounding
so high and trite,
but what the hell,
it was true,
even if my words
weren't up
to the emotion
and thought.

She laughed with me,
because she has a generous heart,
and she nodded,
because I think she knew
what I meant.

Marry life –
alchemy informs –
wed your soul
and the spirit will shine –

But I didn't say that
(thank God).
So we sat down
at a café
over bowls of cold tea,
on a sultry Saturday,
autumn afternoon.

We let the day
and the esoterica
pass,
and talked
all around
revelation's rim.

I
From where did he emerge,
arriving from what supernal realm,
appearing to unfold intact
in front of an astonished classroom?

We are stealing thunder from the future,
he proclaimed to us, one Monday morning,
early September, at the University.
Impressed by the Promethean stride

of his line, I just gaped
and tried to follow
his bold
lyrical independence.

In the students' silence
a waiting like the instant before
a fire catches hold
of the kindling.

How to invent the new, he mused
then surprised himself
into monologue,
Wait I'm getting ahead of myself.

In his relentless originality,
he collapsed information,
Pursuing the transhuman
electric connection, he said.

His speech, synoptic, gnomic,
not entirely sheared toward us,
mind bolting away from the windowless room,
thoughts spearing upward to a point

outside the whitebrick walls.
He said, I want more vision, more sensibility,
but around him the feeling of sharp separation,
as if he were set aside from us.

Words are doing this to me.
A poet must be unwilling to retreat
from possibility. It's essential to remain
equivocal about everything.

II
Once when he sat across from me in my office
I handed him a copy of a book
by Neruda, and said he should turn to the page
called Poetry.

He read, his face deepened into a frown.
Tension exuded from his contracting posture.
His breath became short, wheezy,
his frown darkened into a scowl.

He slammed the bookcover shut
and shoved it back at me
as if I had passed on
something infectious.

That's just fine. Thanks very much,
his voice abruptly mingled sorrow with sarcasm,
I've just read another
goddamned perfect poem.

III

The modernists for all their monstrous egos
were entirely selfless.
Look at how much
they left us.

His digressions more interesting
than the lecture subject itself, in that class
we taught together, The Process of the New,
where we visited with the dead,

surrealists, symbolists,
vorticists, imagists,
dadaists, futurists –
through the tongue of the living –

I believe in divination
through random order.
Poetry is a homeopathic remedy
for bleak desperations.

It's imperative that we risk
mentality –
I mean mortality –
but mentality will do.

So many potentialities
lying dormant before us.

Our class laughed –
They couldn't follow the swerves,
all the bridges gone –
though he trusted something would come.

I have a strategy,
but
I seem
to have lost it.

IV
How do you hold fire,
render it, insist it glow
on the page the way it did
before bewildered faces?

Post modernism, he said,
is Marinetti's Futurism
reborn
with irony.

If you pour enough words
into your head,
eventually they may leak out
as literature.

Manifestos, manifestos,
there should be manifestos
for everything,
even for going to the bathroom.

The chalk in his hand snapped
when he swirled
enigmatic designs
on the blackboard –

I like that sound.
It means
something
is happening.

And he paused –
as if a flash felt only by him
had directed him elsewhere
again.

Ah I may be straying
too far today,
he reflected
(to whom?).

I went too far over the borderline,
though – he looked into the faces,
recognizing where he was –
we have to get there

to come back
from the other side,
collecting
new data.

V
In the forest on the campus north side,
we took a walk after class one afternoon.
Early October. The flowers and trees
still bloomed. In midconversation

he stopped, stooping
to touch the petals
of a flower
I couldn't name.
He called to it,
speaking softly,
gazing with respect
and fondness

for its indelible
discretion.
He studied more
of the flowers

that warm day.
In his eyes
wonder at what thrives
at perception's edge –

Nothing ends, he said,
when he straightened
and stepped back
to the path.

You see,
no one can truly say
how many worlds
coincide.

VI
He read *Prufrock* to us,
a Monday morning in November,
his voice hesitant,
unnamed loss haunting the rhythms.

We are abandoned, he implied,
we are all left behind finally.
He looked up from the page,
seemingly staring at nothing.

And began, God and his angels
lived on a planet
that was once close
to earth.

We started to orbit away
and our noise filled
the airwaves
of space.

Soon God and his angels
couldn't hear us,
they couldn't pick up
our calls.

The angel Gabriel hailed
into his cosmic telephone,
Hello hello
who's out there?

Where are they?
What is she
what is he
trying to tell us?

God and his planet
of angels
drifted farther
and farther away.

Then he resumed reading
of the mermaids' song
and drowned voices,
in his tracking hermetic chant.

Christopher, you'll never be fully caught
here or anywhere,
the flames
would singe us.

VII
In Trevor's café,
a quiet campus pub,
I watched him
crash —

Inward, haggard,
selfprotective, evasive,
he sipped strong coffee,
and lit a cigarette.

I'm trying to quit,
he said as if to apologise
for a crime
he once committed.

We said goodbye
on the walkway,
vowing we'd meet
someday for a drink.

He paced off,
head bowed,
a nervous zigzag
toward the trees,

his deepest contemplation
and kinship reserved
for everything
that eludes the human.

*

I was being interviewed in Toronto
when the journalist asked,
Are you an optimist?

I'm uneasy
with that kind of question,
and mused, but didn't say –

I love the morning's redglow
glaring sun at heartening noon
darkening in blue dusk
radical silence at night
the night that isn't Armageddon black
but bodied with stars
upon stars
the unwritten unheard unsaid
things trembling like incantations
about to begin –

*

Ulysses invented Homer
Socrates argued Plato
into being
Jesus created Mark
Beatrice gave birth
to Dante
Satan found Milton
willing
to make his case –

Hamlet thought
of Shakespeare
needing the way
to meditate and murder
before a crowd –

Don Quixote hovered
around Cervantes' mind
until that traveller
conceived
the windmills
of a spiritually depleted
Spain –

Ahab forced the *Pequod* on
to sink
Melville's career

letting him rise again
only when he had drowned
anonymously –

Anna Karenina dreamed
Tolstoy
to help her flee
her tragic fate –

I
I loved foraging in small bookstores
on cul-de-sacs.
It was easy to imagine myself
some genius among pages and words,
all books my companions.
I'd meditate on the mysteries
of vortex titles and names:
in our time, The Waves, Wolfe, Mann,
Crowds and Power, Kafka,
One Hundred Years of Solitude.

A time when I'd wander
through a single book –
The Cantos, mad Ezra's sea –
then go off hunting
for books about that word
intoxicated
seemingly lost generation,
which didn't seem lost to me.

Once I asked an elderly greyhaired lady,
in a shop so hushed
I thought I'd paused
in a shrine,
for Hugh Kenner's *The Pound Era.*
Humming happily,
she thumbed spines
in the Political Economy Section.

Perplexed, I asked,
Pound?
Ezra Pound?
The poet?

She wheeled toward me
and fluttered a pale hand
to a stray strand of hair.
Saying

O my,
I thought you meant
the British Pound.

We laughed, as if we shared
the secret of books,
each edition like a hieroglyph
of universal contact,

an image vessal,
talismanic
of transforming,
unifying thought.

But I've changed, and the stores
have changed.
The moveable feast
is an allyoucaneat smorgasboard

in megastores with megabooks,
CDs, DVDs, videos and games.
Along aisles signs announce
Oprah's Choices, Award Winners,
The Next Best Thing, Read Canadian,
Our Picks –

This could be an outbreak
of premature grumpiness,
a grouchy, touchy dislike
of epic merchandising.

Yet truly – I'll use Hemingway's
pivotal code –
I don't feel the rage
waged on matter,
on theme pen paper screen keys –

Think of Henry Miller, Anais Nin,
Robinson Jeffers, HD and DHL,
scouring malls
desperate, livid for truth,
and I'm sorry,
I can't see it –

I can't imagine portly Wallace Stevens
hoo-hoo-hooing and ric-a-ricing
toward yet another autobiography
by some unimaginably rich,
vapid entrepreneur.
Maybe I love strangeness too much –
cutting curiousity – unruly solitude –

Bellow, Berryman, Lowell,
Sexton, Mary McCarthy,
Williams (WC and Tennessee),
Rilke and Roethke –

generations reduced to items
in a catalogue, abandoned

but not in the way
Gertrude Stein might have meant it –
just filed off
somewhere,
destined
for remainder bins.

II

Late: the moon's arc asks you
to leave this life behind –
the dark brightens – in melancholy retreat,
unseal, summon your self

into the book
the moonlit sentence
the heartpulse saying

(though not to any ear,
more to itself
than to anyone near)

follow, if you dare,
toward the margin –

the nail of the word
the pierce of the page
into
your eye

*

Why I have trouble with so much contemporary verse:
the widespread application of an ironic ideology,
too much discourse and not enough intercourse,
too many lines falling away from the dance,
the lack of divining, the forgotten beat
of the heart seeking other hearts,
denied gnosis that we are ardent,
constantly thwarted, the absence
of desperation,
all the missing diction
of our journey
back to paradise –
I can't read much of it
because I can't bear
the omission
of the soul singing
to be whole.

*

What became of the fathers
who left us
without mercy
or reprieve?

What became of the fathers
who led us
with their rage
for right?

Huddled together on alien sands,
wounded, grieving in the night
by banked firelight, we pray
we may wake from war

and the calling
of the dead.
We have dreamed a dream
and there is no interpreter of it.

But my son
remember
I shall give my ships
to you

I
I couldn't stop dreaming
of the war.

Night after night
marching troops, the red beach,

falling friends, breached seawalls,
bullets tearing into flesh,

the smell of spent shells and powder,
black smoke, shrapnel, tracers, screams.

II
We were committed to war,
soldiers conscripted
by an elusive command.

We were battling an enemy
who grew stronger
no matter how well we fought.

We were always under towers
beneath walls and gates
waiting for their fall.

III
Last night
across the horizon
of my dream
came the vast armada,

a vivid array,
catamarans, sloops,
sunrays, squareriggers,
schooners, barks.

Tarsmell, rigging creak,
masts like flag standards
in the wind, longships,
caravels –

a mermaid herald
carved
on a finlike
prow –

A thousand ships
bearing down
on the beach,
and out of the boat

settling first on shore,
stepped my father,
who was young again,
powerful and tender.

In the volleys
he handed out coats,
in miraculous colours,
speaking out to us,

The war is over,
the betrayals are done,
justice will return,
love is unbroken, come home.

IV
Along the beach
voices answered
and asked,

Who redeemed whom?
Whose ships
are these?

Who made
the peace
and the healing?

We heard
a cry
from the ships,

The war is over,
come home.

V
Old men, made new,
had come back
for their sons –

fleets sailing
from deep harbours
and anchorages

to restore
the world
of their fathers.

*

*...on what coasts of the world
have we been tossed?*

I touched her face in the car.
The softness was new,
weaving around her eyes.

It's here, I said, complete
between us, I see moonlight
weave into your hair –

The promise of starlit space
turned into the brightness
from arclight and neon.

That light may be a gift
blessing us but is it
is it –

Before you opened the cardoor
and left, I asked you,
Tell me

what you see
when moonlight
weaves.

*

You've been searching for mysteries
not to solve
but to enter
You've come searching for mystery

Adrift on water, stilled fragrant air
Scent of pines, a sound from island caves
Images in the liquid mirror fade

Who was here

The mask turned away
like a ship's sail
set for the unknown

This is the tear
in reality
through which
you pour

A voice that whispered
among the ruins
and stones of a temple

When two souls meet in dreams
the planets no longer compete
but mend
to end misrule

Look back, the ancient city is deserted
Still the wind needs pines to speak
The waves seek your shore to caress

Love come close
you were meant
to rise
and sing the sea

*

Animals watch us,
planets look down.
Trees crane
to catch our song.

Clouds comment,
Earth prepares a stage.
Flowers audition
for the human rage.

Here's the secret
making life pause:
we are radical magi
remaking the laws.

Light bends,
night puts darkness first,
rain floods,
to inspire our thirst.

Chemistry of mind and flesh
makes catalysts fire:
the universe senses
the ambition in our desire.

*

The soul should be left
slightly open like a window –
when the nameless knocks
it may be ready

for the rattled glass,
the crack that could break
wider –
being denied.

*

I feed on solitude –
defiance like rawness
knows community
may be transient –

more hope than fact,
loneliness the stimulus
while machines spur us
to global extravagance.

*

The car ahead swerved, jammed off the road,
skidded and stalled like a stunned animal
caught in an unexpected trap
on trashstrewn grass.

Spring, a cloudless sky,
birds singing, life everywhere
like triumphant royalty
reveling in its restoration.

I slowed my car and saw the driver looking pale,
startled. He shook himself in disbelief.
I drove on thinking
how can you love this, smashup in freshlight.

How can you love poptins and burgerwrappers
on green grass, a hubcap dented and bent
like an abandoned communion plate
among the flowers.

The heart must sing no matter what comes.
Welcome disaster, celebrate this crash,
endure the awful glory of the sun
illuminating cars and trash.

I geared down at the stoplight,
and peered in my rearview mirror
at the frustrated driver stuck behind,
gunning his machine, grasstufts flying like grapeshot.

Amor fati

Nietzsche said these words
should brand your spirit.

Amor fati

Love what scathes, gaze joyfully
on suffering, ruin, wreckage and waste.

We may never see God's face, or the soul's tip,
but we can return to desperate zero,
our freedom
to love

the grinding squeal –
tires
digging
into April earth –

Amor fati

Let me tell you: in several short weeks
my wallet was stolen, my pc ate my writings,
I became ill with appendicitis,
peritonitis lashed in, and dazed I almost died –

later during an ice storm my car slipped off
the road, tilting down into a ditch –

it went on and on
a run of miserable luck –

and I kept repeating to myself
I'm not supposed to regret this
or rise above it
I must feast on it, savour it.

The light turned green. I glanced from the mirror
to the road, and, without knowing why, pressed down
on the gaspedal. My car lurched forward
as if gleeful it wasn't stuck there.

Soon I couldn't see the other car
or the junk sprawl on the lawn.

Embrace these

every shock irony accident agony
every loving transient touch
every mistake escape faltering apology
every smashed bowl that was an heirloom

Embrace these
Embrace this
Embrace

I
It was the summer when my father went to the hospital
to sit by my mother, weak after breaking her leg,
and did the morning paper's crossword puzzle,
both saying hardly a word to one another.

It was the summer when my uncle went to the hospital
while my aunt withered, disappearing into bafflement,
and he spoke with a gentleness not typical of him,
and stayed all day, until she slept.

My father found, after driving miles in swarming air
under the scalded sky, a mere kiss
on my mother's cheek seemed to penetrate straight
through to brittle bones.

My uncle drove to the hospital across town,
took the elevator up to palliative care, and watched
over the woman he'd loved for forty years.
Her mind eaten away, she didn't know him.

The two men often had supper together
on parched nights, drinking
too much red wine, telling one another stories
about their wives, and their day.

II
It was the summer when loved ones needed canes,
sometimes reaching abruptly for invisible support,
until you extended a hand,
or leaned beside them.

It was the time when fathers refused help directly,
proclaiming, I'm fine,
but cried out nevertheless
like ones making hesitant first steps.

It was the season when I saw the people I love
forget the scripts of their lives, like actors
in a musty play relying on cues
that had long ago lost their link and meaning.

III
He watched and waited,
while she faded.

Who's that?
she asked her nurse.

Your husband,
she answered.

I have a husband,
she said.

Yes,
he said.

And I have a wife.
You.

She smiled,
a sweetness

in
her puzzled glow.

IV
He pushed her in her wheelchair
around
white corridors.

Pushing slowly,
he gazed down
at her thin white hair,

and watched her hands
resting folded in her lap,
their frail stillness.

She was silent
a good deal
of the time.

Sometimes he saw
her red swollen leg
through her green gown.

And he remembered
the night long ago
when he first saw her.

The good would come,
he thought,
in small things now.

V
It was the summer when my father and uncle cooked
for one another and reminisced about wars
they'd fought and observed,
a total of seven between them.

It was the time when the heat hung over them,
their postures slumped, their gait became uncertain,
and at night in apartments too large for one,
they preferred to watch old black and white movies.

VI
Who is it
you're talking about?

she asked
him.

Your daughters,
he said.

Yes? What are
their names?

He told her,
saying each slowly.

Yes, she said.
I have daughters.

VII
There was a moment,
he explained that night
over a drink at his home,

when her face relaxed,
and the bones
softened,

and the age
went out
of her features.

She was young again,
very beautiful,
for a time.

My father listened,
and they talked,
while autumn came,

fall heatswells
intense beyond
the predictions.

VIII
I saw these two men
in their homes, and the different ways
they cared for themselves.

One, newspapers cast on the floor,
underwear and socks stacked on tables,
as if everything after her was chaos.

The other, his rooms immaculate,
so orderly it seemed he expected
an inspection from a higher authority.

They lived on the same street,
saw each other every night, and talked
about the news, and their women.

IX
I wish I'd had benedictions
and prayers to help.

All I had were the phone calls
and the hours spent listening.

During breaks between words, in wards,
the unsaid passing –

How naked, humbled we are
in the face of this love.

X
Milkweed and petals,
fireflies guide us
over the field.

Touch
from duskwind,
invisible kiss –

light beside us,
our forms
disperse.

Fireflies
guide us,
into the fields.

*

You must stay well.
Don't walk under cracking bridges
which need repair.
Don't pause under rotting trees
whose limbs waver in the mildest wind.
Don't wander along badly-lit streets
where drivers are reckless, almost blind.
Don't disregard warnings on packages.
Be sure to sleep and dream deeply.
Stay clear in your mind.
Be sure to wear a coat when the forecast
spells the fierce arctic discharge.
Beware of words that coax you
toward distracting shadows.
Don't succumb to those illnesses
of the soul.
Stay sound.
Keep yourself ready
for conversation, laughter,
affection and stories.

*

Leaves burn on my front lawn.
Maple tree as if rawnerved, skinned
in dusk's blue imposing air.

Brown grass with green streaks,
where lush, reminiscent
of our brief victorious spring.

I'm missing you,
your cleverness, energy, youth,
seductions, humour,
overcome by this obscure mourning
inadequate, incomplete –

Leaves surround the trunk
as if they yearn for branches,
lament the loss of roots.

Tree bones grope
like the fire's smoke toward the dark,
for what the wind will surely bring.

I
I switched on the light
coming home late after
errands and Tae Kwon Do.
The night blacker than usual
and my children strangely worried
by knowing –

It's almost like magic, Katie said.
Like the start of the day, Thomas agreed.

The hallway, spiral staircase,
sideboard, mirrors,
had brightened suddenly
like surrogates of the sun,
as if we had permission to glow
whenever we wished.

II
It's a fragile revelation,
I explained,
feeling very much the teacher,
Not so fired
as what lights up
your souls.

I don't understand
what you mean,
Katie fumed,
nearly frantic,
I'm only ten
years old.

I'd wanted to tell them,
show them,
something
more
than the uncanny
flick of a switch.

III
I saw their souls
when they were born,

light flickered
at skin's edge,

their shapes
radiantly stirred

when they stretched
and palmed the air,

lashes fluttering
over filmy eyes.

IV
That night, Thomas asked,
while he undressed
for bed,
Dad, can you
really see
the soul?

Always
from him
the grounding
question,
the abrupt cut
to the essential.

I almost answered,
yes
I once saw yours
at the rim
of your eyes
like the sun

emerging
round
the world's curve,
if you could see
the morning
from space.

You grasped
toward hands
and words,
the warm presences
hovering like
the glaze of shades.

We were amazed,
your mother and I,
by the numinousness
your new world
kindled
in us.

V
I thought I saw the soul
then roused, awakening –
knowing my own
as if for the first time
like an ember's spark

in the waking
a mending,
connected warmth
restored,
darkness diminished,

the soul searching
for other souls,
eternal
kinship
revived.

VI
After Katie and Thomas fell asleep,
I paced around the house,
sleepless again,
thinking, thinking
too much,
turning down the lights.

In my mind I saw
my grandmother,
Kathleen Brady,
born Katrina Romanick,
that strong stubborn woman.
She died
soon after the twins

were born.
In her decline
we watched
her soul prepare to fade.

Bigboned, tall, vehement –
difficult and independent –
she once cracked a plate
over my father's head
to resolve
an argument.

He was simply wrong,
she explained,
he had to know.
The child of abusive stepparents,
she marched out of their house
at twelve, in Nelson, B.C.,

and hiked alone through the Rockies
to Calgary, where she took
on an Irish identity and name,
reinventing herself,
and read so much
no one knew she was self-educated.

But when she began to die,
the glare from this imperious
opinionated spirit
started to retire –
shuffling off
to its home.

Her striking light
withdrew, sidling
silently away,

moving as if offstage
behind the curtain
to an appointment elsewhere.

I remember
how we asked,
Where had her energy
gone?
All that brightness –
Where?

VII
Sometimes I feel I'm saying goodbye,
to what, I'm not sure,
yet the grieving deepens,
grooving into me
like ridging cracks
in a tree.

This mourning,
sorrow like a perpetual autumn,
leaves forever falling,
may be for the hooked
sense that I've left
too much behind,

as if I've forgotten
to turn out a light
in a room
or dropped a vital piece
of identification
on a halflit street.

This thought apprehends me:
I may always feel your hand

slip from mine,
watch my home empty,
hear the door shut
when you leave,

be rooted
in silent
spaces, still rooms
marked
by the char
of love's searing.

The Buddha said,
Let it all pass,
never attach yourself,
attachment brings suffering,
and there is no end
to grief.

But I find sorrow
stays now,
it cores into my psyche –
my marrow
its seed
and soil.

VIII
I thought I saw the soul once,
glittery and fine
like the beads of rain
that brilliantly appear
around the textures of clothes
people wear

if they've left
without an umbrella,
after sunrays
spread
like a golden mandala
from behind fading black clouds.

And I saw the soul go
leaving sprinkled memory
like the starlight we know is
only the myriad reflection
of their first billowing
shimmer and intensity.

Now my children laugh,
cry, quarrel, ask questions:
when they turn on the light,
our house
switches back
to brightness.

They yammer
and scramble upstairs,
shedding clothes
along the way,
heading
for their bedrooms,

disagreeing,
muttering,
in the familiar safety
of the things
they think
won't change.

Darkness returns,
our fears,
and dreams
of radiance,
mostly unknown
to one another.

A DAUGHTER'S SONG

I see imaginary things
in beautiful dreams.

I become the unicorn
who insists on the sun.

I become the angel
who makes evil run.

I fly like the bluejay
who never asks why.

I see beautiful dreams
in imaginary things.

*

We worked on his homework together,
and he didn't get it,
no matter how we tried.
Maybe some stubbornness
wouldn't let him follow the words.
He seemed blank,
tired, frustrated,
strained –
and I looked at him
heartsick
that I couldn't help –
this unsettled core
in him –

Later in bed
before my son
finally slept,
he said
there was a hole
in him.
He often felt alone,
though he knew
I was there.

On in the night
the heartsickness
and sense
of helplessness
wouldn't leave me.

I knew this was it
stripped of myth,
metaphor,
structure, form,
simile, story,
image,
art itself –
this was it

Goodnight
I said
to the dark
and the page –

Goodnight
to silence –

and loved him
all the more

*

Anna my neighbour came to my door last night.
She leaned against the frame, her back to the snow
drifts in their whirlwind,
crystalline grace.

Her eyes were swollen, red –
from a cold, she said,
and she blurted how
her husband had deserted her.

She was alone with her two girls,
what was she going to do?
Why had this happened?
Now, just after Christmas.

I couldn't answer,
except to sympathize,
and to sound awkward,
and invite her in.

The snow's eerie night glow
fringed her anguished face.
She said no, she had to go back
to her children.

The old holiday song
began playing in my mind,
absurdly, out of nowhere:
where is the wonder?

What is the wonder,
the portent and pledge
at this time of year?
Or so I remembered it.

Anna left. I watched her cross
the snowbanked street.
She stepped carefully on the ice,
her shoulders hunched

against the cold,
going home to face
the questions
and the hours.

The snow surrounding her
shrouded
our street
in beauty.

On my front yard
the white mounds
and dunes
were beautiful.

The trees
snowdraped
and icicled.
Such beauty.

What was it
that was meant
to link all this
together?

*

On my bedroom door
I found a sign
scotchtaped there
after my children
had left
for their mother's

Katie
Thomas

all

              love

    you

I read
the words
over and over,
first one way
then another

All love you

All you love

A house
these rooms
this paper
this pen

Something in me unconsoled
and inconclusive, a reclusive disposition:

an isolate heart,
unreachable –
182

until the day comes
when I read
the sign again

and hear
their knock
at the door –

*

Darkness crosses our star
like a hand blotting out
light's possibility –

Break from warmth –
ritual,
expectations of the sun –

and solitude
takes me,
welcomes me back.

Solace, embrace, rooting dark:
I'm directed toward
the whispered word, sounds,

cosmos and stranger voices,
what won't be known
any other way.

*

Working on these pages
in early evening,
snow clouds impending,

I felt a breeze
sigh through a window
I must have forgotten to close.

I checked the window
and found it shut.

But the curtains rustled
like candlelight in stirred air

and again I felt a breeze
like a caress
saying

you are inside
everything –

*
Come
Sunday

in my mind dancing
before the light

with all the might
I have left

*

Walk in the forest
walk and want nothing

the still tree
whiteness and silence

you go blank like the snow
silent like the tree

you move, released
now, to dream

*

Days so raw
your bones
receive every atom
of air –

days so fine
your nerves
pulse –
somewhere, a new star

*

I flow out, and flow back,
with my children, their impatient bustle,
shouts, rages, demands, and whys –
with my neighbours, and the heavy snow
dumped deep this year on our driveways –
with the last cool glass
of beer –
with you, and your worried hopes
about tomorrow –
free and obedient, I return –
and flow out, and flow back,
cooking, cleaning, driving, working –
write – love – and pray –

A FATHER'S SONG

If I had the gifts
to give
they would be

a seashell
to remind you
of tides,

the womb
beat
that is

the unceasing
movement
of yourself –

a rose
to recall
the heart

how over time
love's progress
sometimes heals

what ego
and anger
divide –

a bird
to remind
your soul

how it's free
to return
or escape —

a tiny silver box
sealed
with the instructions

never to open
to remind you
life is mysterious

each of us
a song sung
by something else —

finally
a poem
like this one

my way
of saying
goodbye

1995-2004

BY THE SAME AUTHOR

A Climate Charged
(1984, reprinted 1985, 1987)
The Solitary Outlaw
(1987; second revised and expanded edition, 1995)
A Tremendous Canada of Light
(1995; second revised, rewritten and expanded, edition,
under title *A Canada of Light* (1996)
Outage, a novel (1995)
*Light Onwords/Light Onwards (*essays, editor, 2003)

Printed in October 2005
at Gauvin Press Ltd., Gatineau, Québec